AUGUST REVERIE II:EPIC

FANTASY ART ADULT COLORING BOOK

ISBN-13: 978-1720722670
ISBN-10: 1720722676

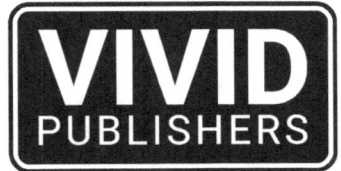

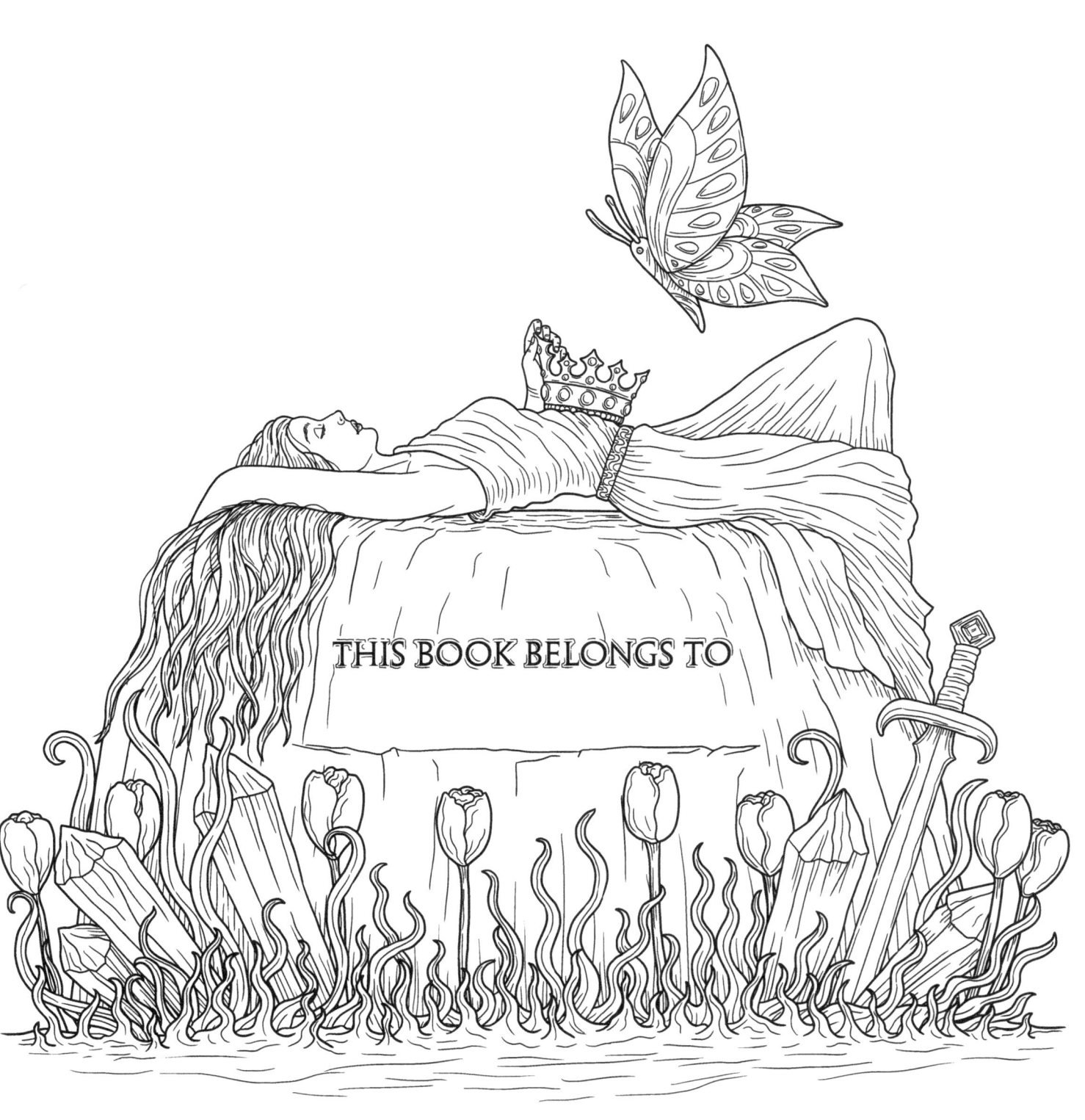

THIS BOOK BELONGS TO

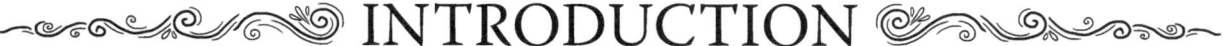 INTRODUCTION

Thank you for purchasing the second book in the 'August Reverie' adult coloring book series: EPIC. We garnered a lot of positive feedback from you, the colorist and the coloring community as a whole for the first book August Reverie, so we thought we would create a second one to follow, only pushing the envelope even more in the realm of fantasy art this time.

We have a selection of twenty four plus detailed fantasy art illustrations here for your coloring pleasure.

All art is hand drawn & line art shading is included as a guide to add shadowing & lighting.

You can use any coloring medium from pencils to markers as long as they have a fine tip.

A note on the use of markers: Even though the illustrations are printed one per page, to give additional protection please place a thick paper or cardboard beneath the page you are coloring so that the ink will not bleed through to the next page.

Subscribe at our website to get a FREE PDF Sampler featuring pages from our other adult coloring book releases! Plus, news on discounts, free pages, contests and more!

 www.vividpublishers.com

Finally, we would love to see your completed art. You can reach us at:

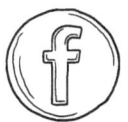 fb.com/VividPublishers

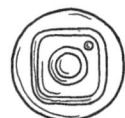 @VividPublishers

Also, we welcome you to join our Facebook group to share your art, see other colorists' art, enter exciting contests plus more!

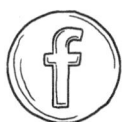 fb.com/groups/VividPublishers

Thank you for your continued support and interest in our adult coloring books. We hope you enjoy coloring the pages as much as we did creating them. Happy Coloring!

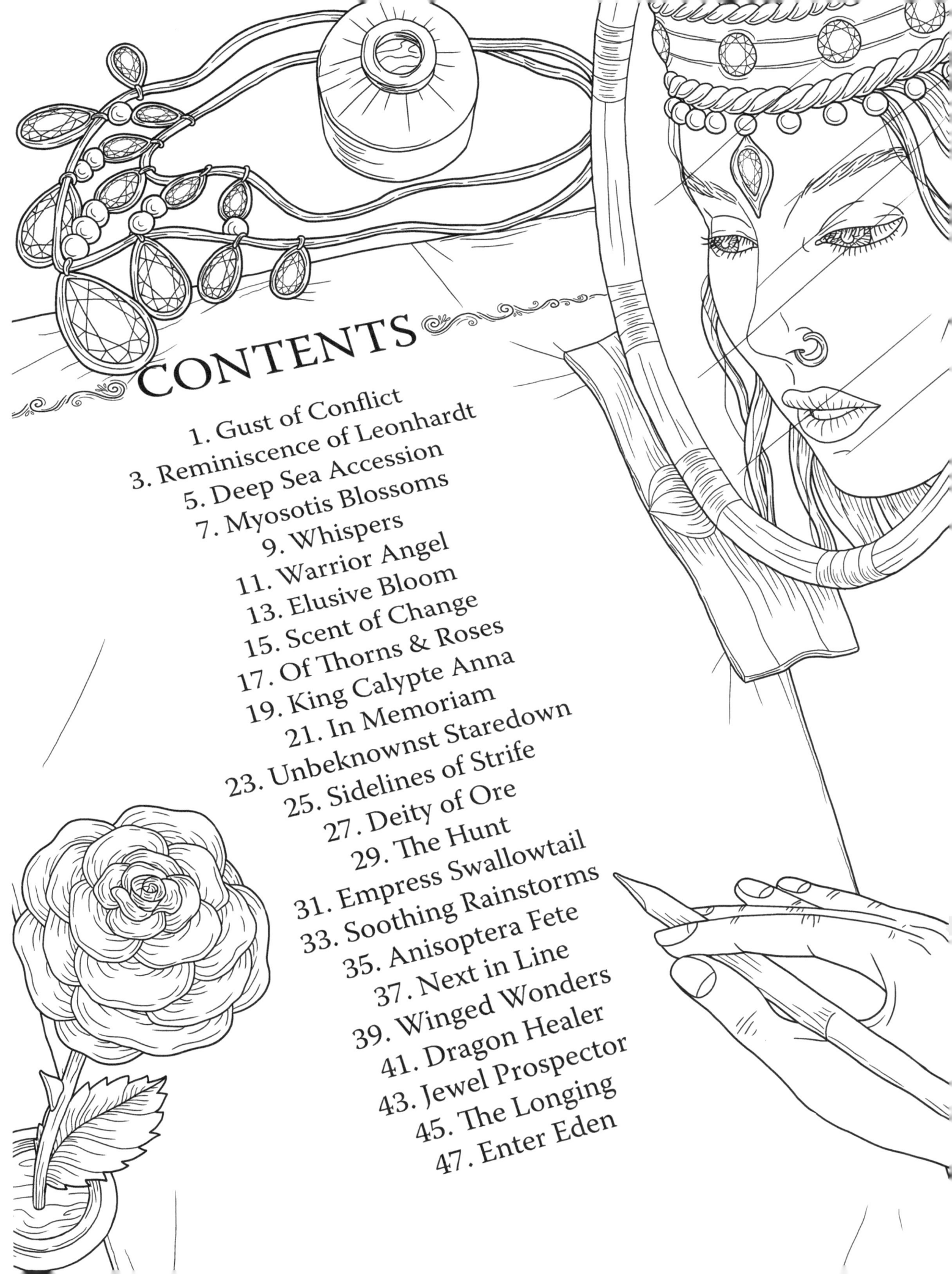

CONTENTS

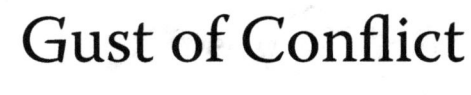

Gust of Conflict

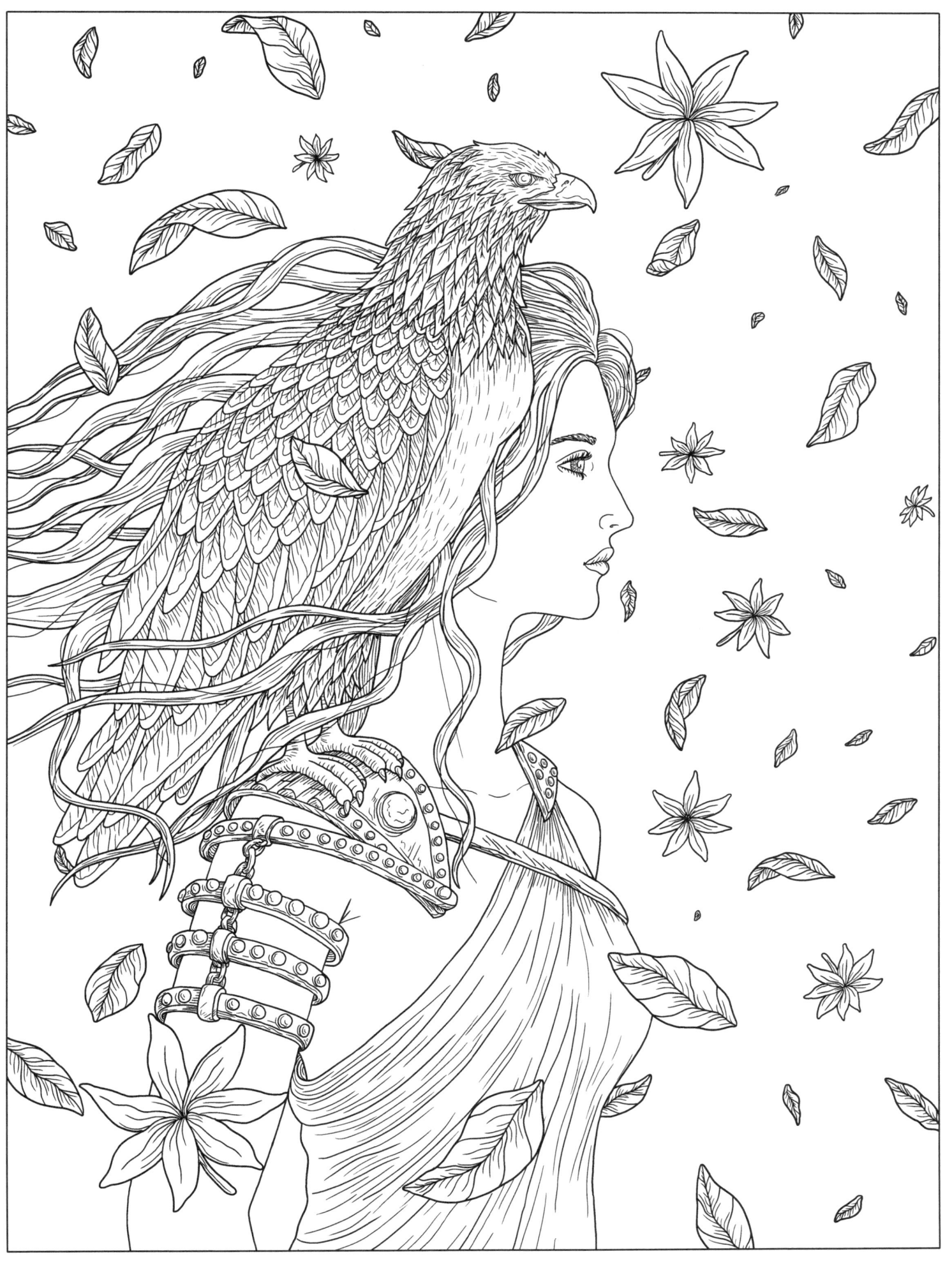

Reminiscence of Leonhardt

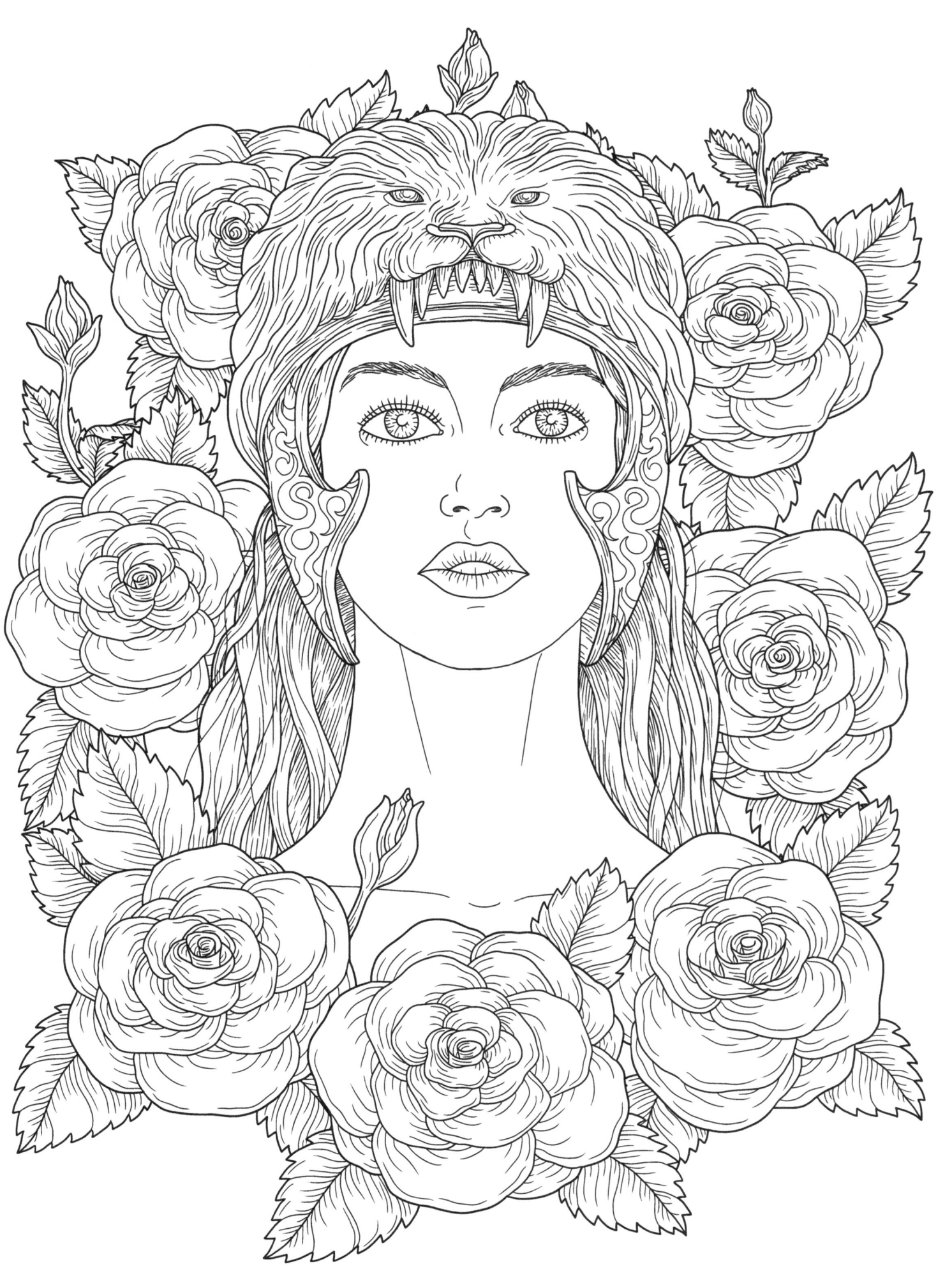

Deep Sea Accession

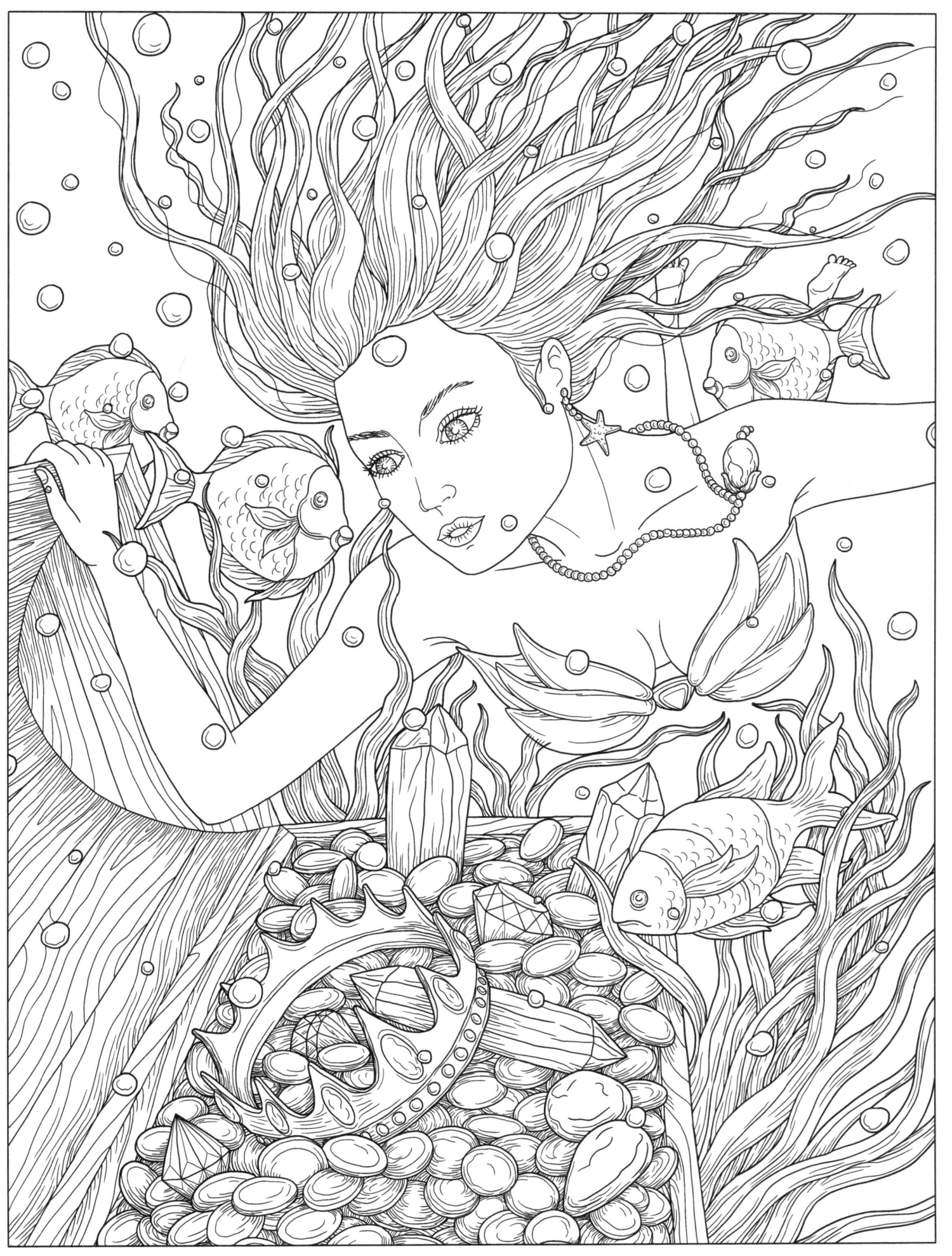

Myosotis Blossoms

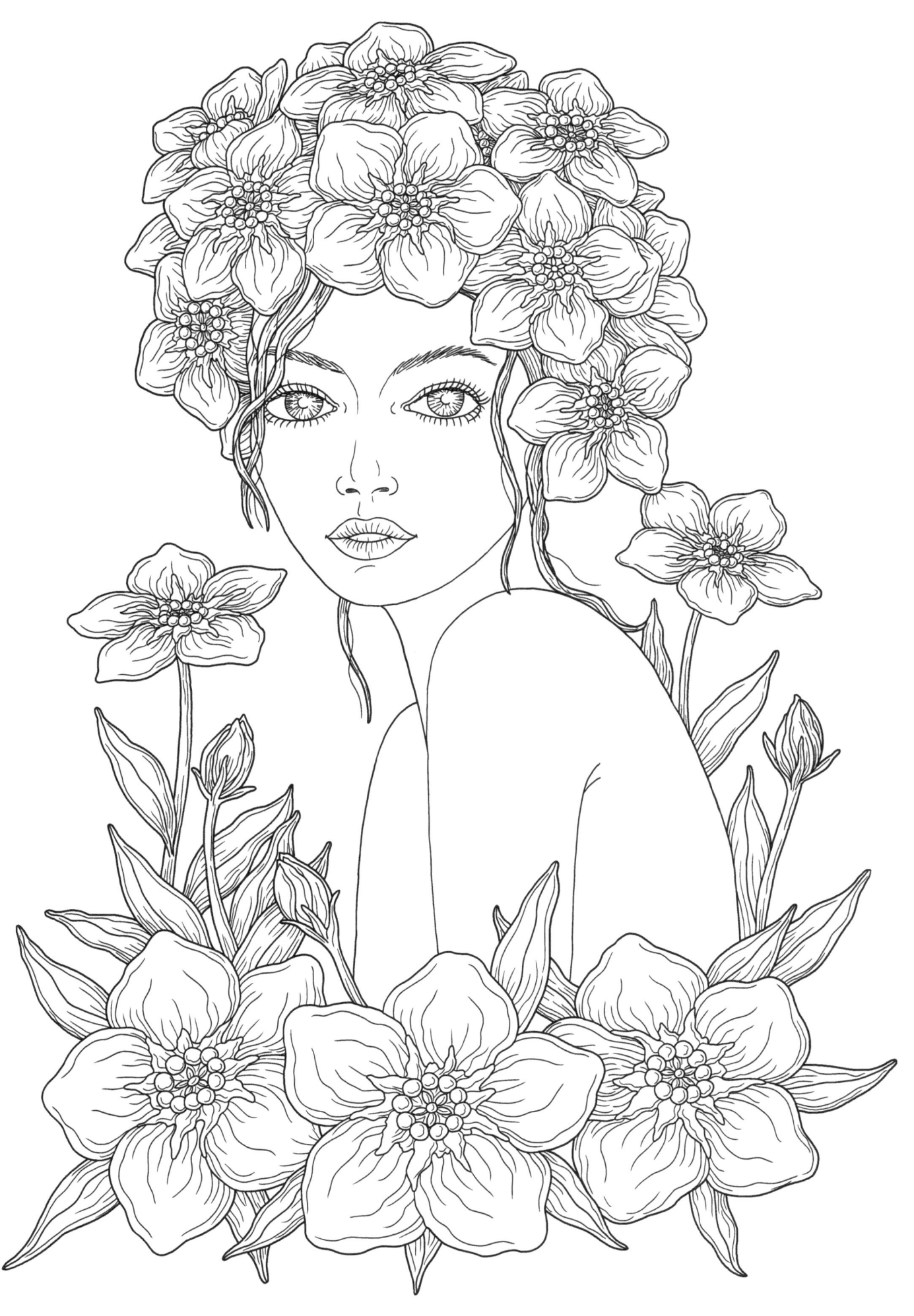

Whispers

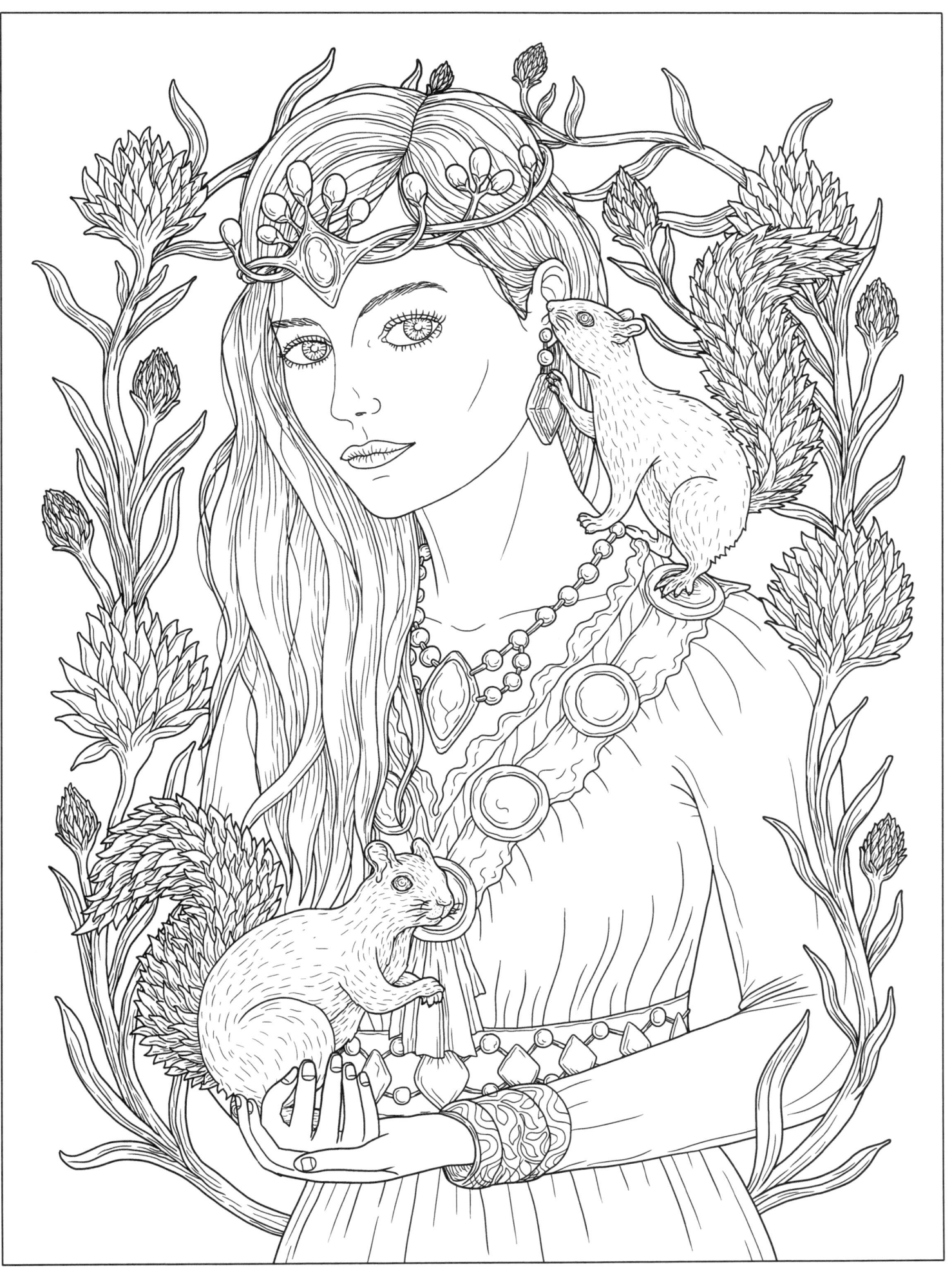

Warrior Angel

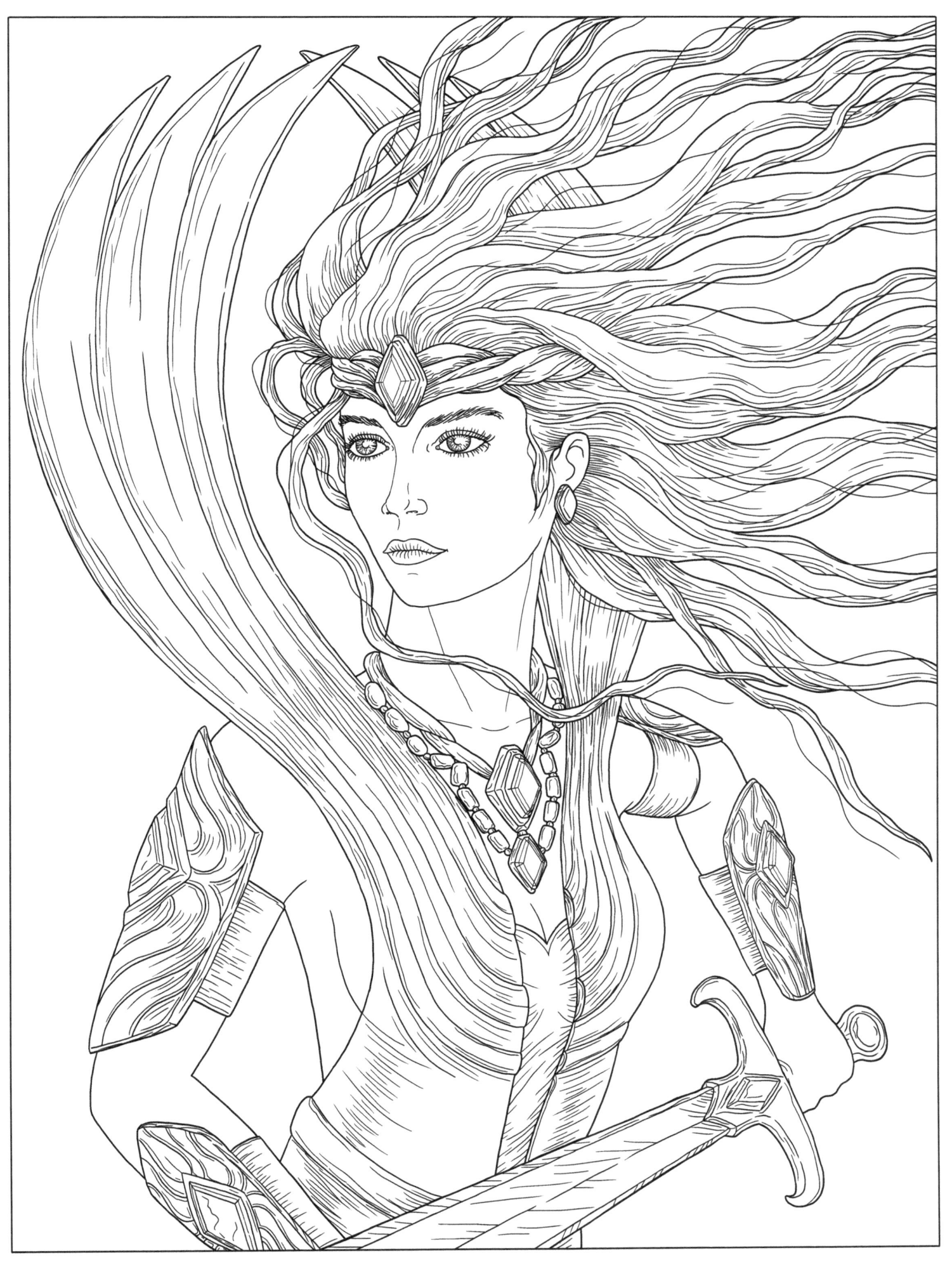

Elusive Bloom

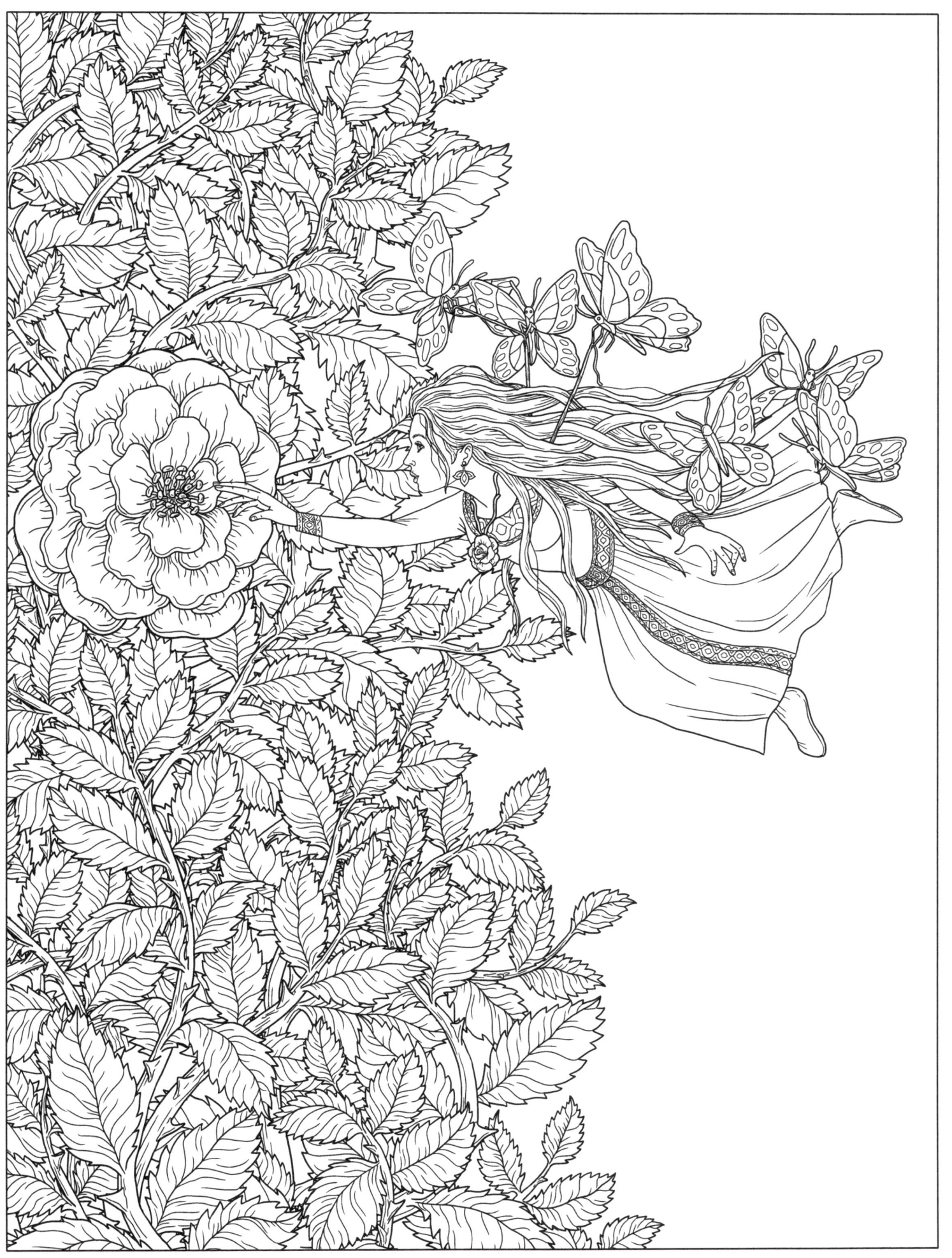

Scent of Change

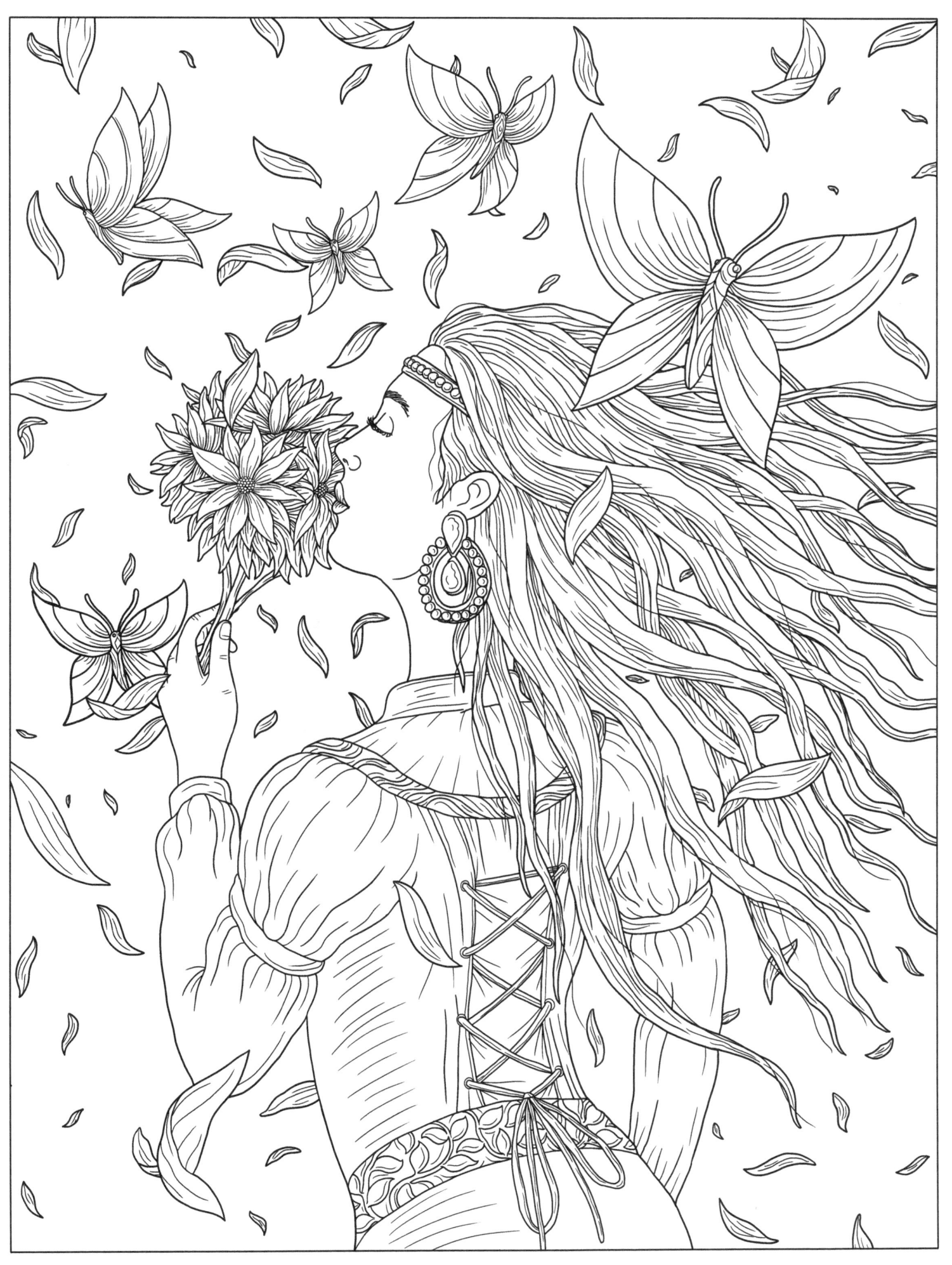

Of Thorns & Roses

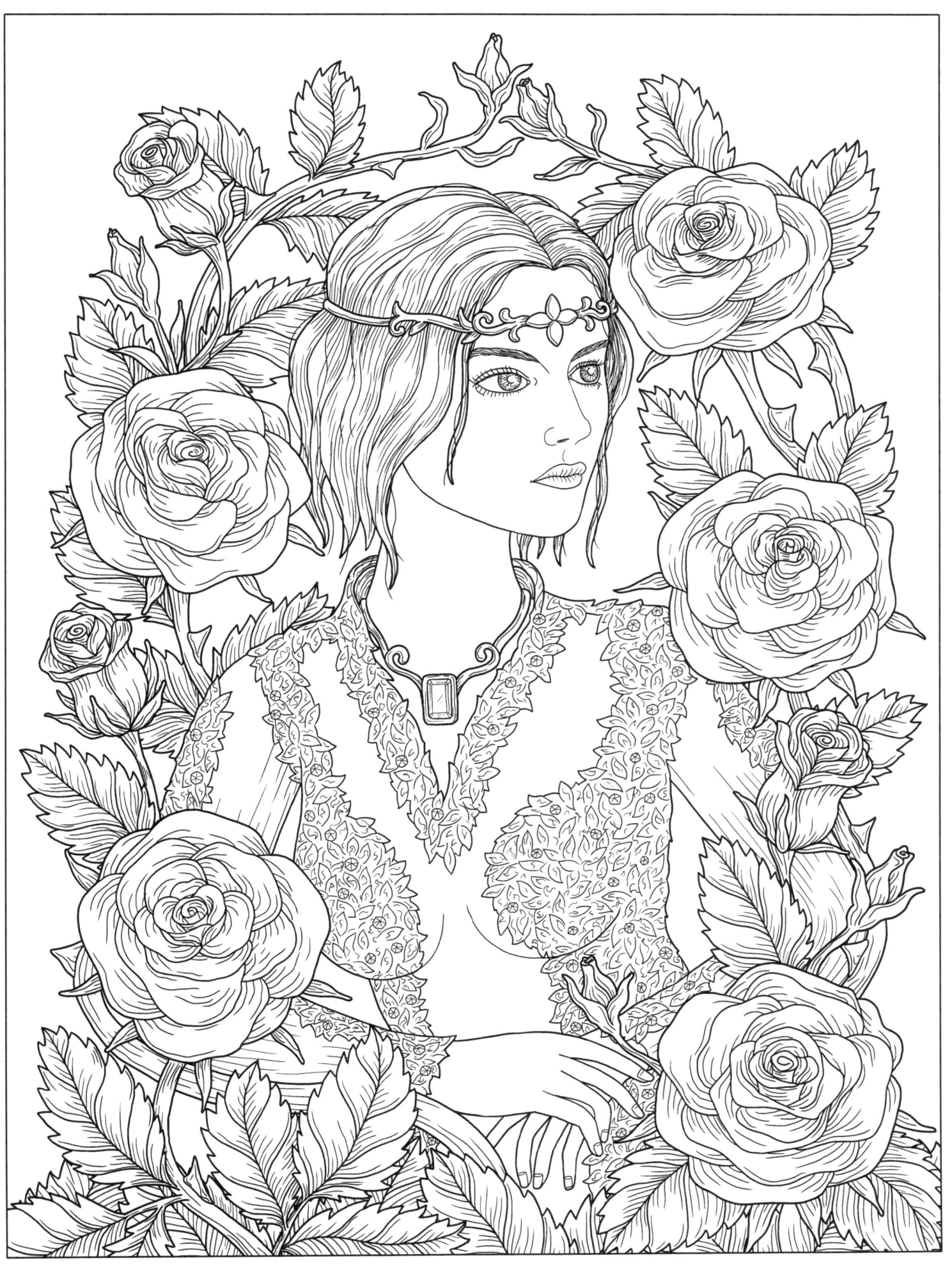

King Calypte Anna

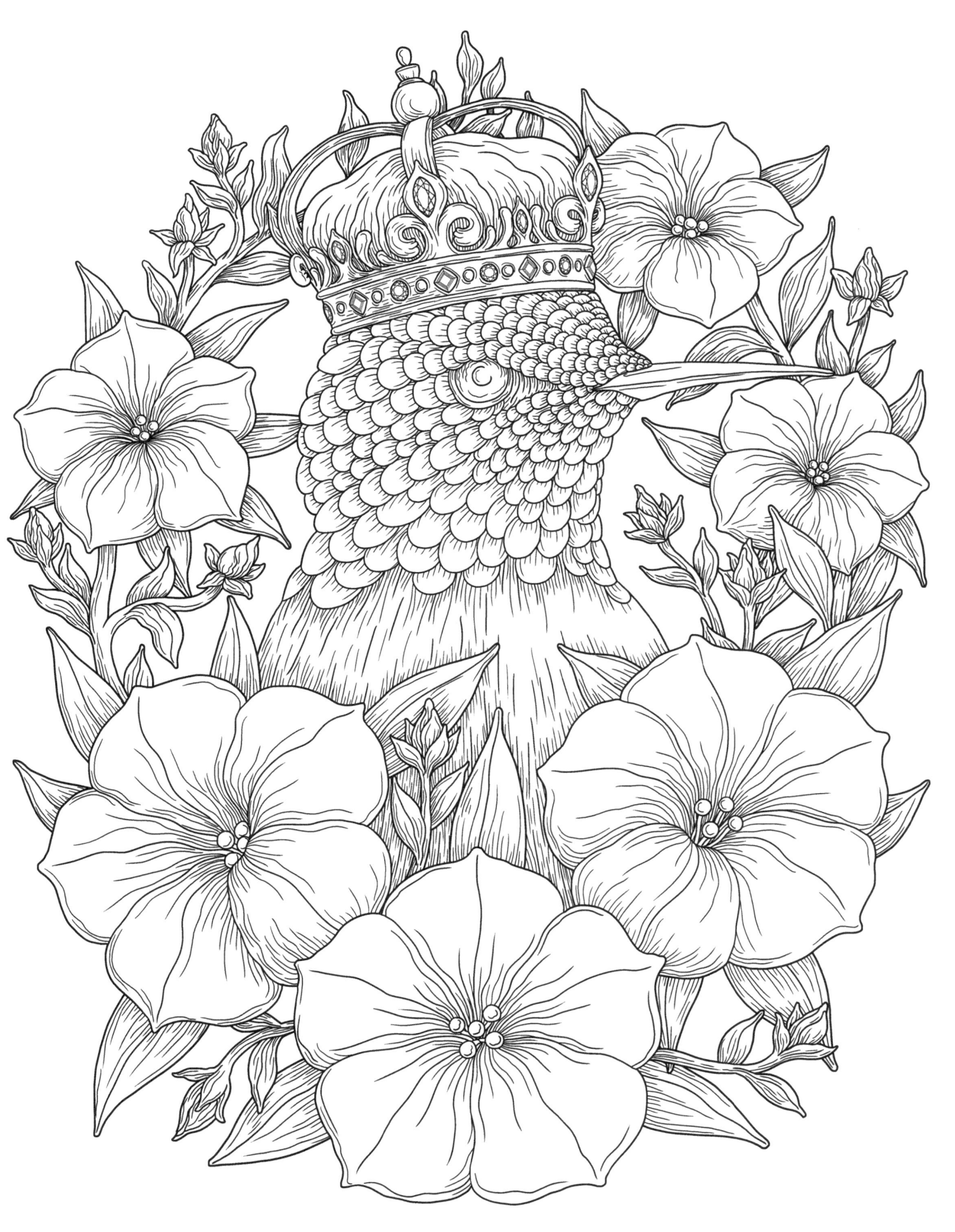

In Memoriam

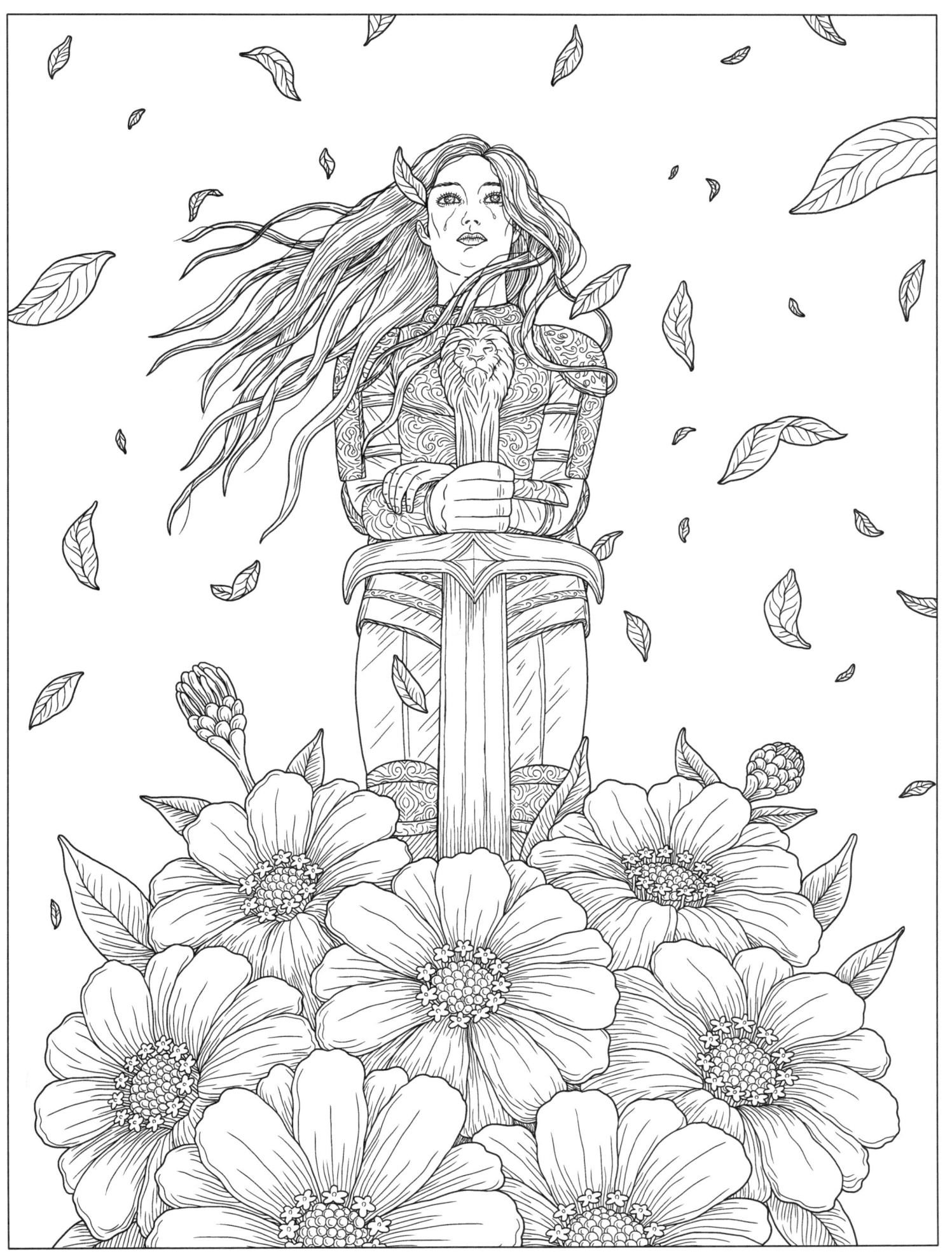

Unbeknownst Staredown

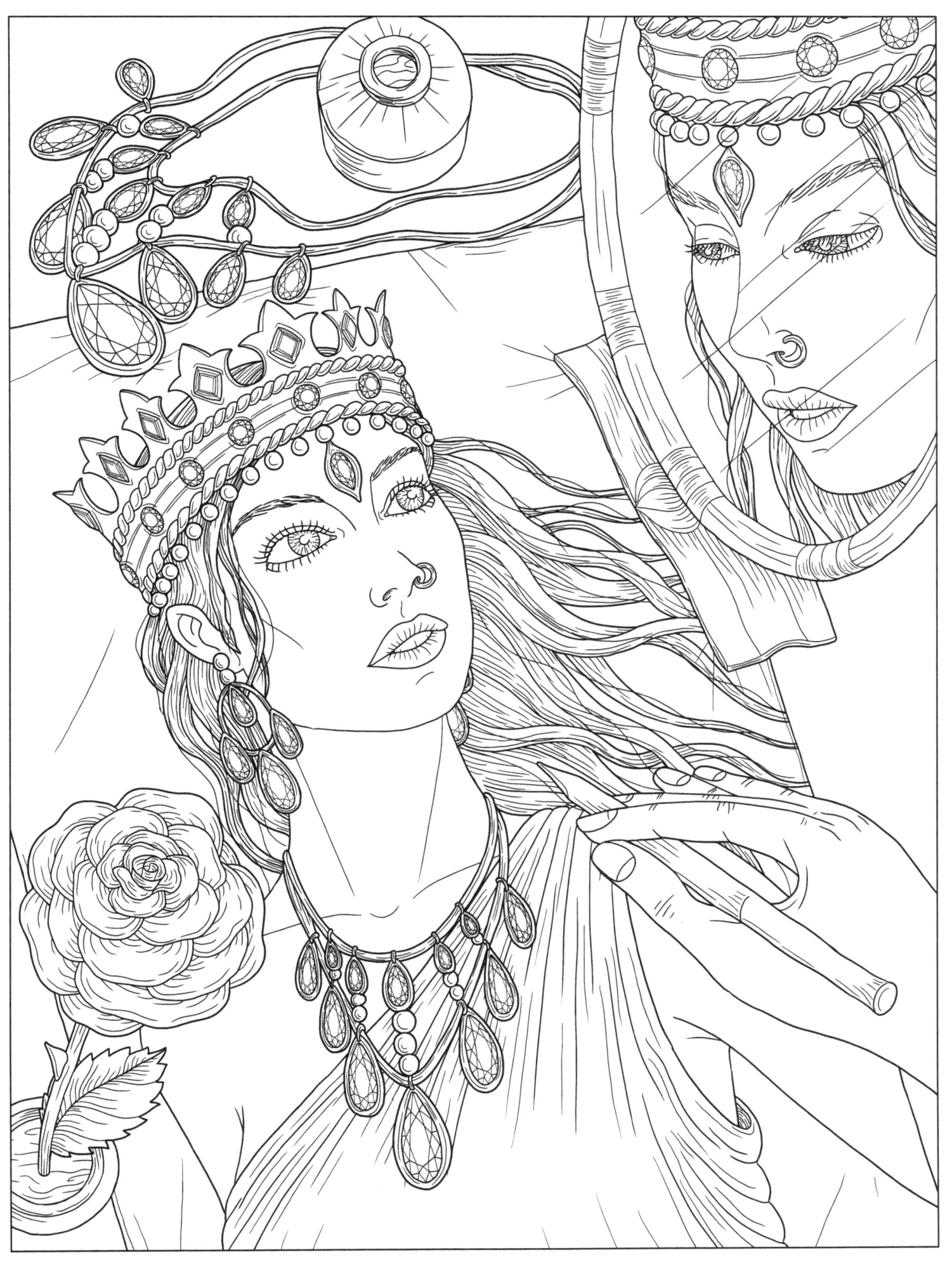

Sidelines of Strife

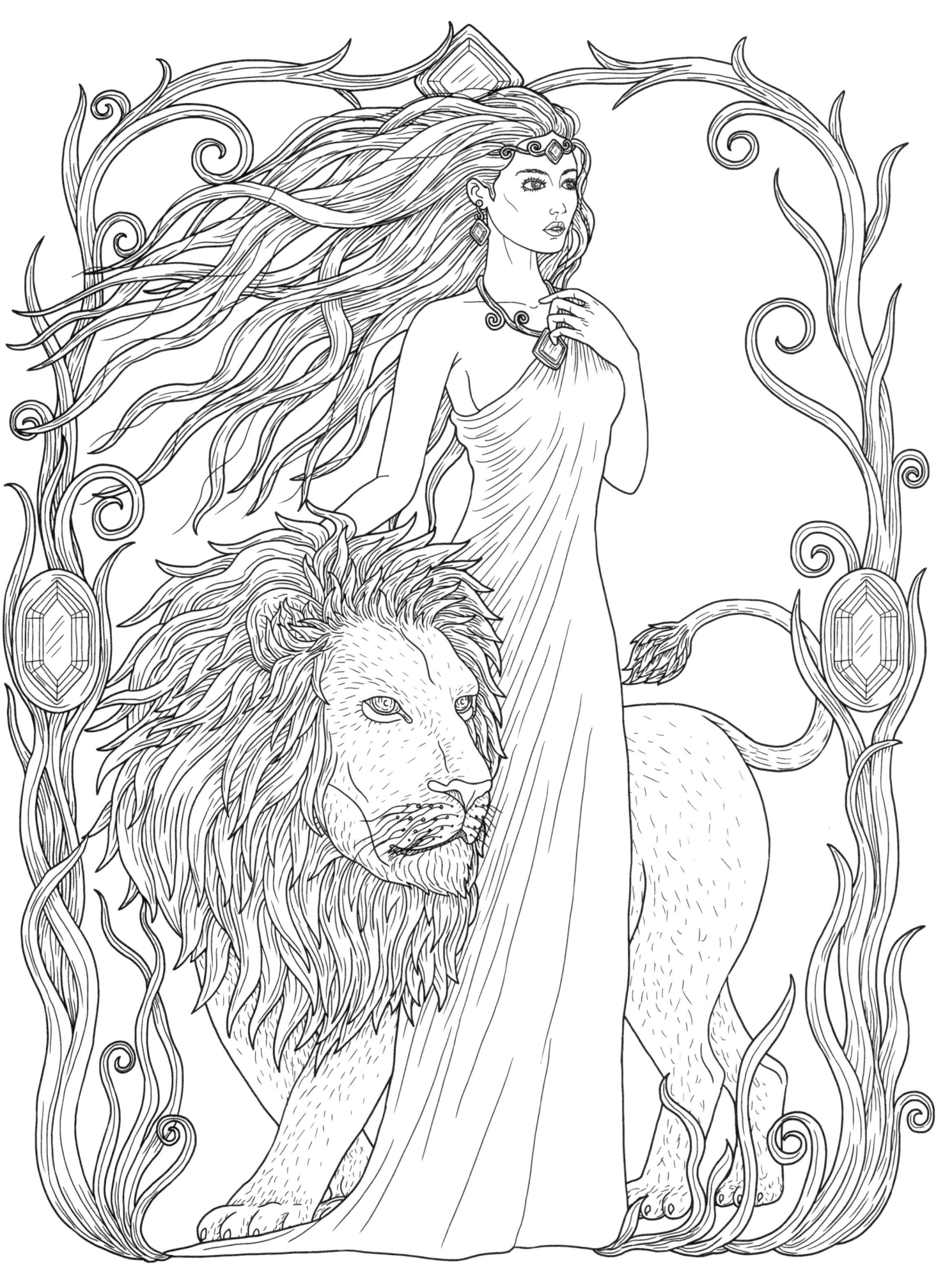

Deity of Ore

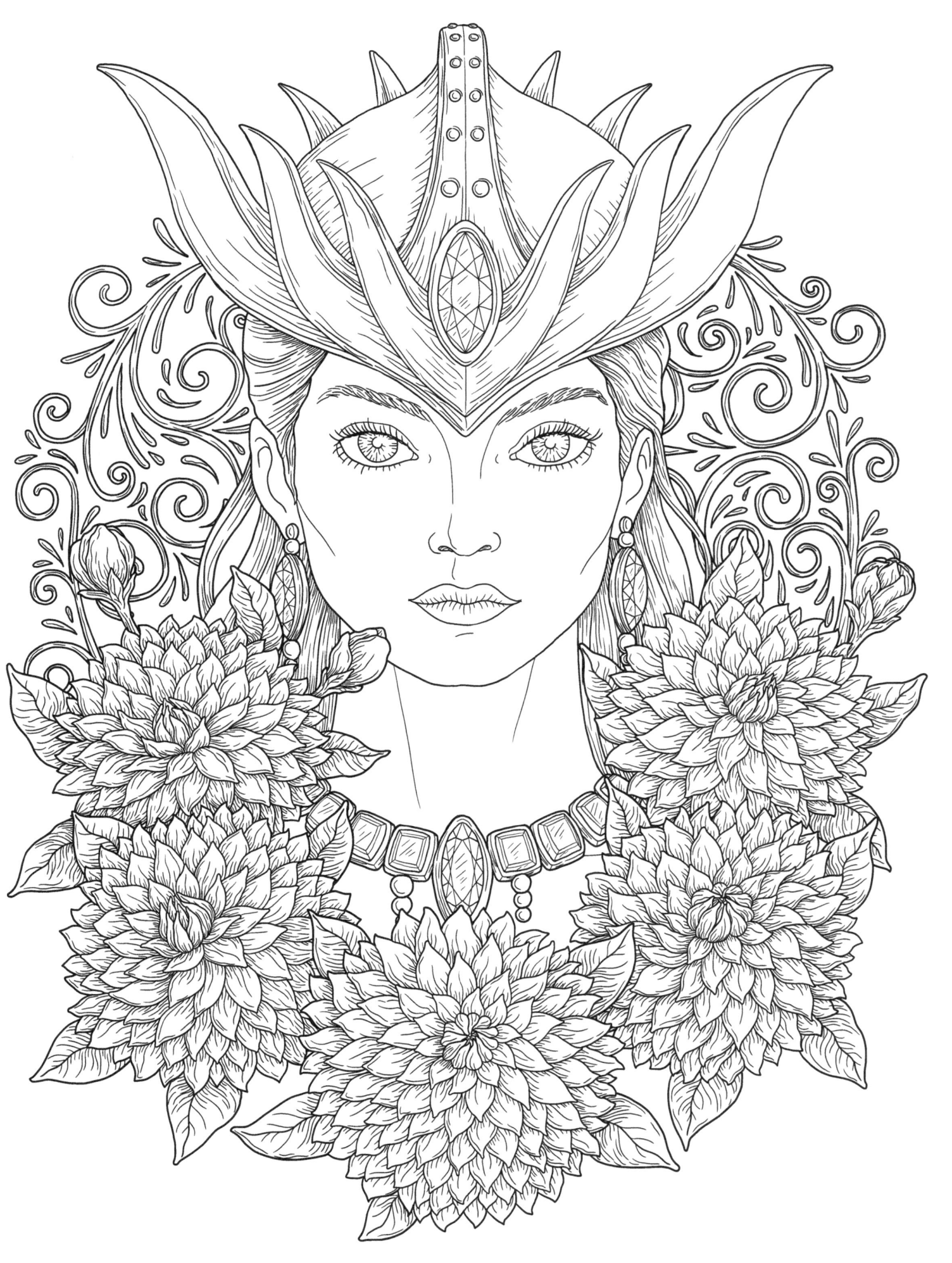

The Hunt

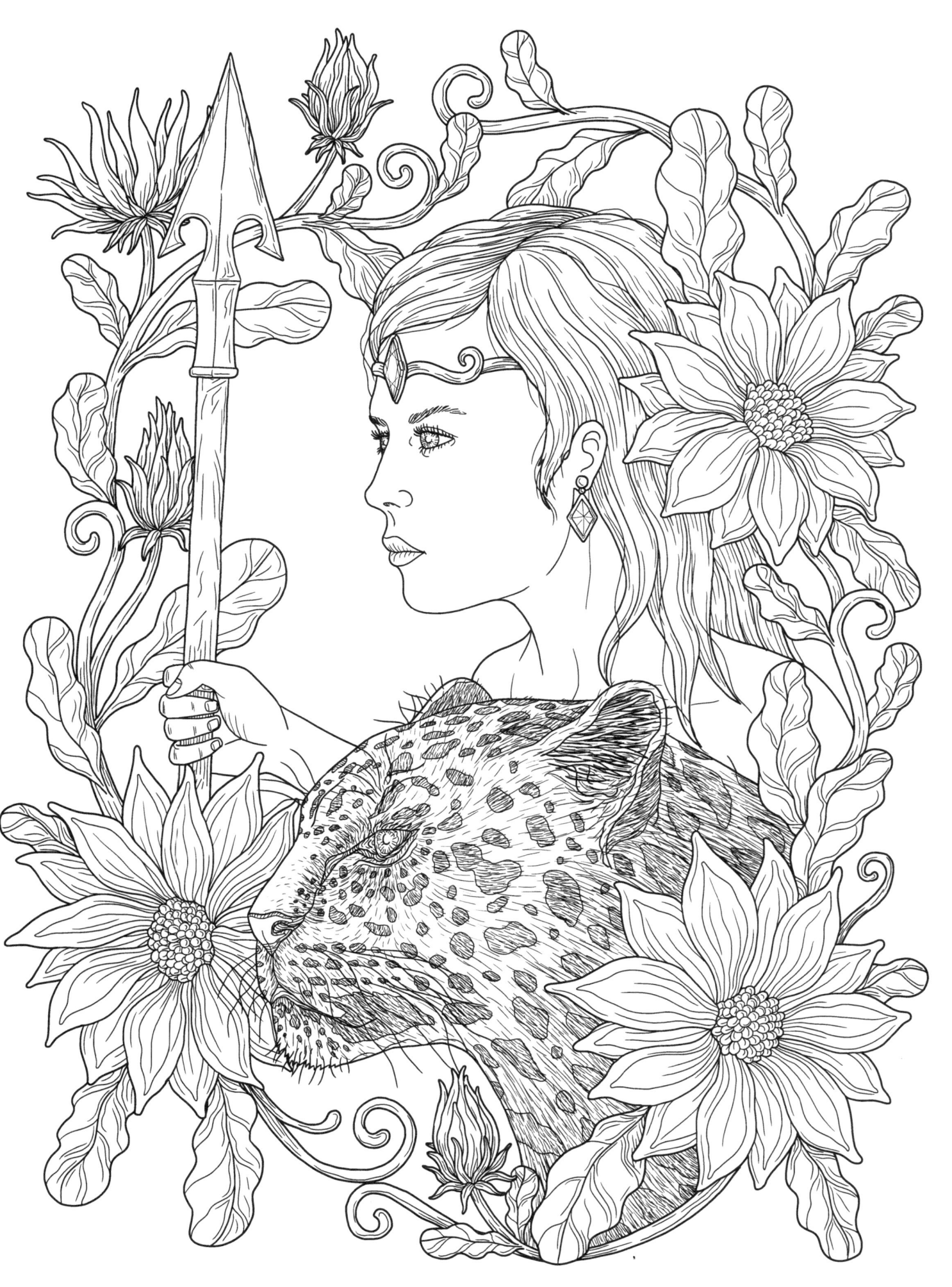

Empress Swallowtail

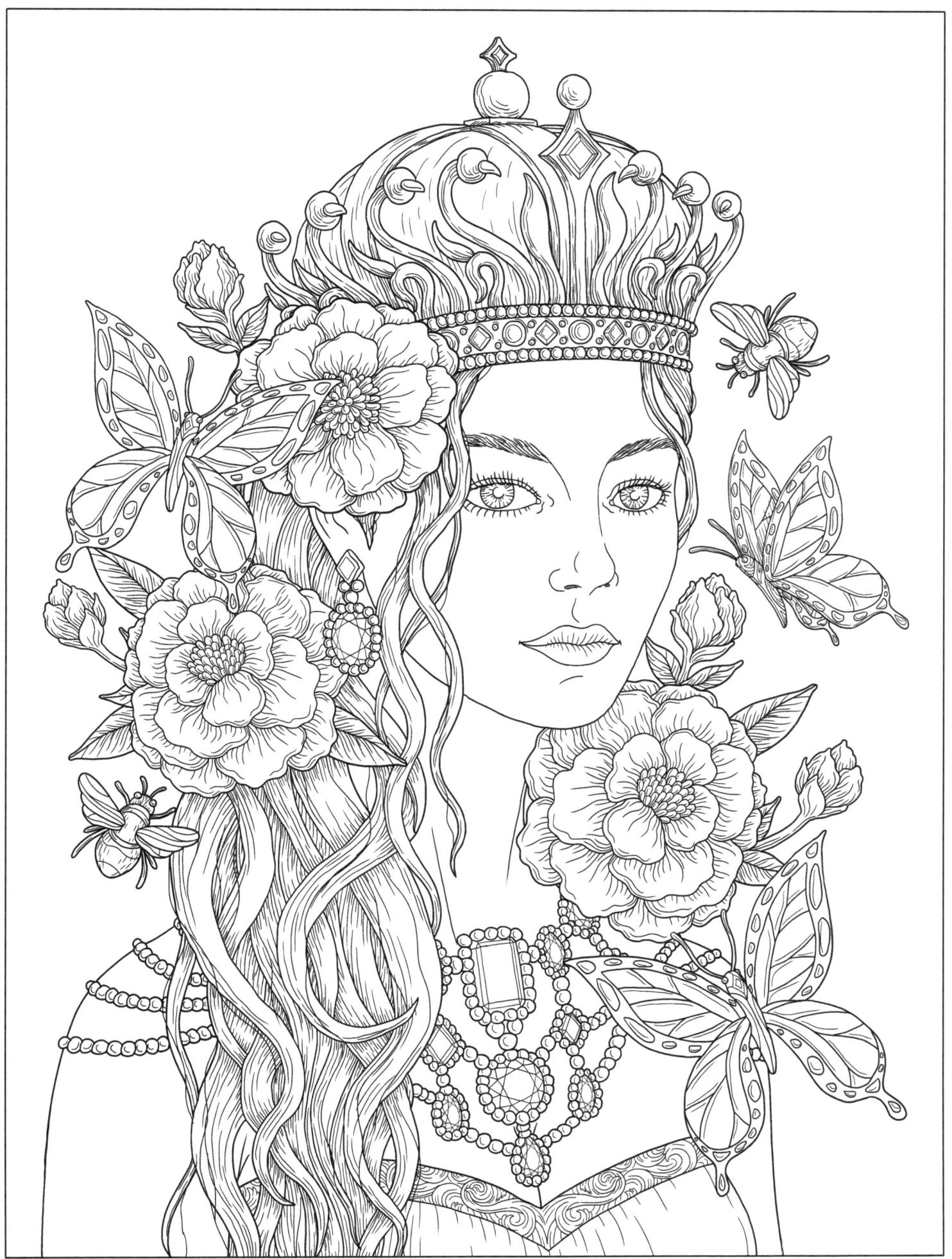

Soothing Rainstorms

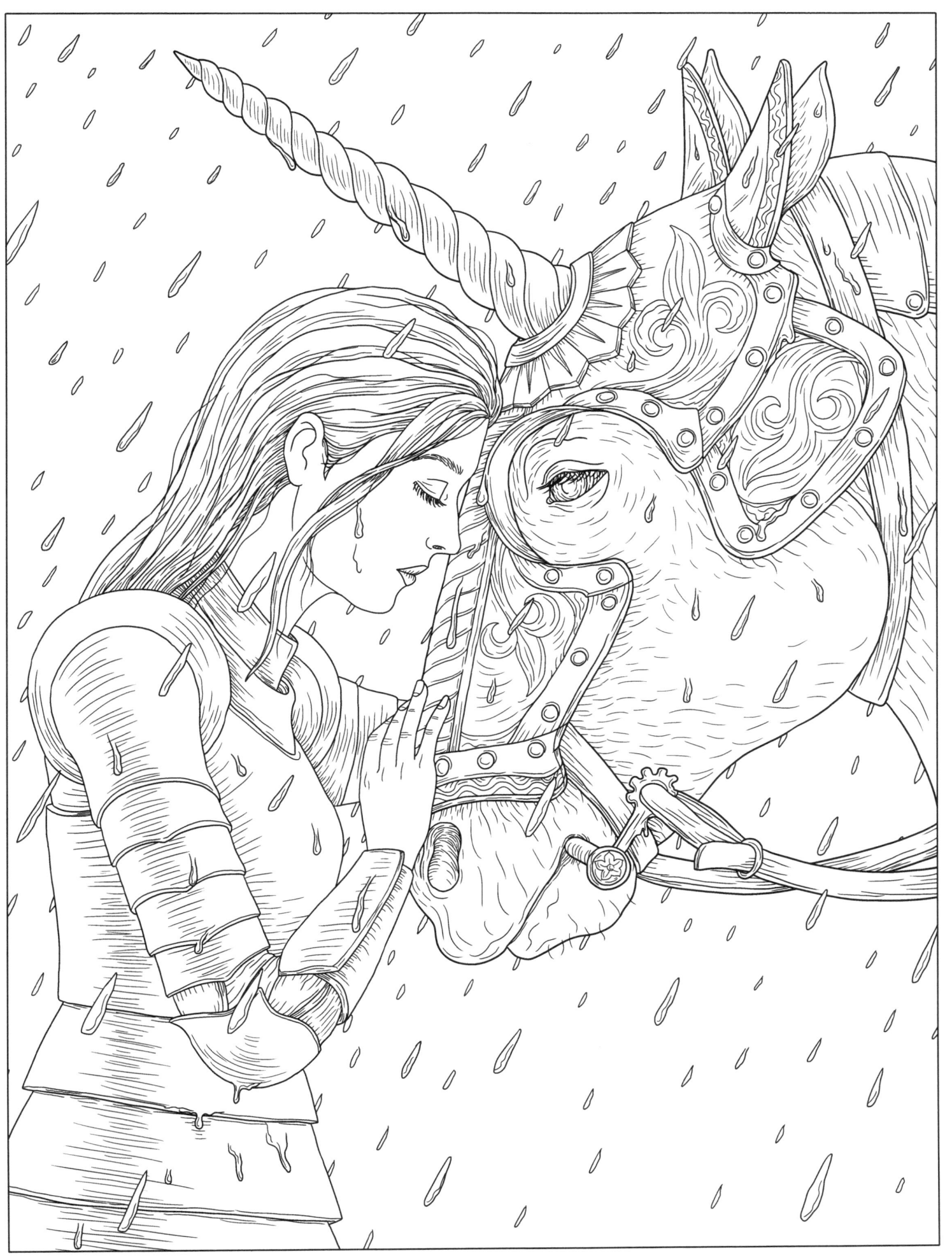

Anisoptera Fete

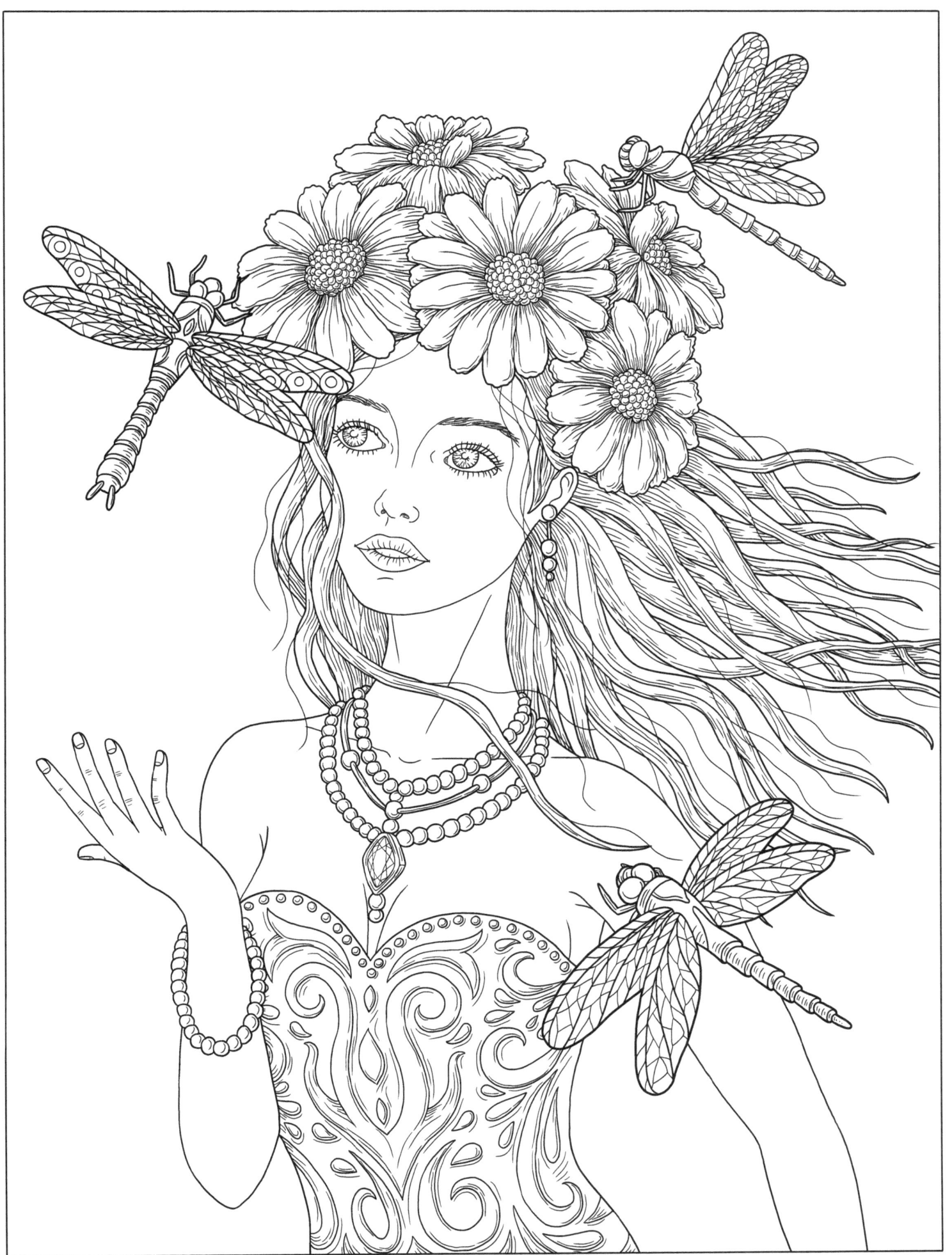

Next in Line

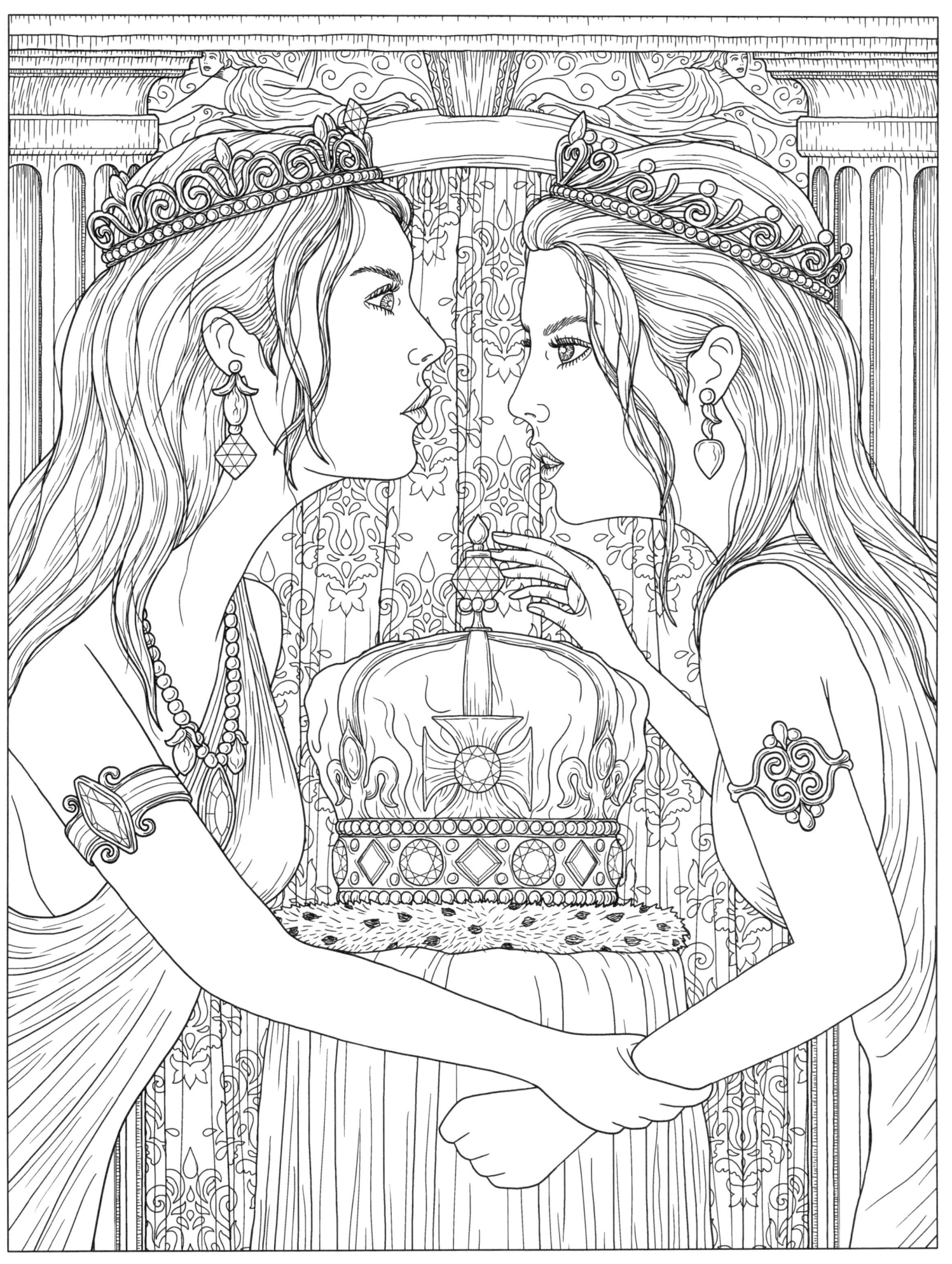

Winged Wonders

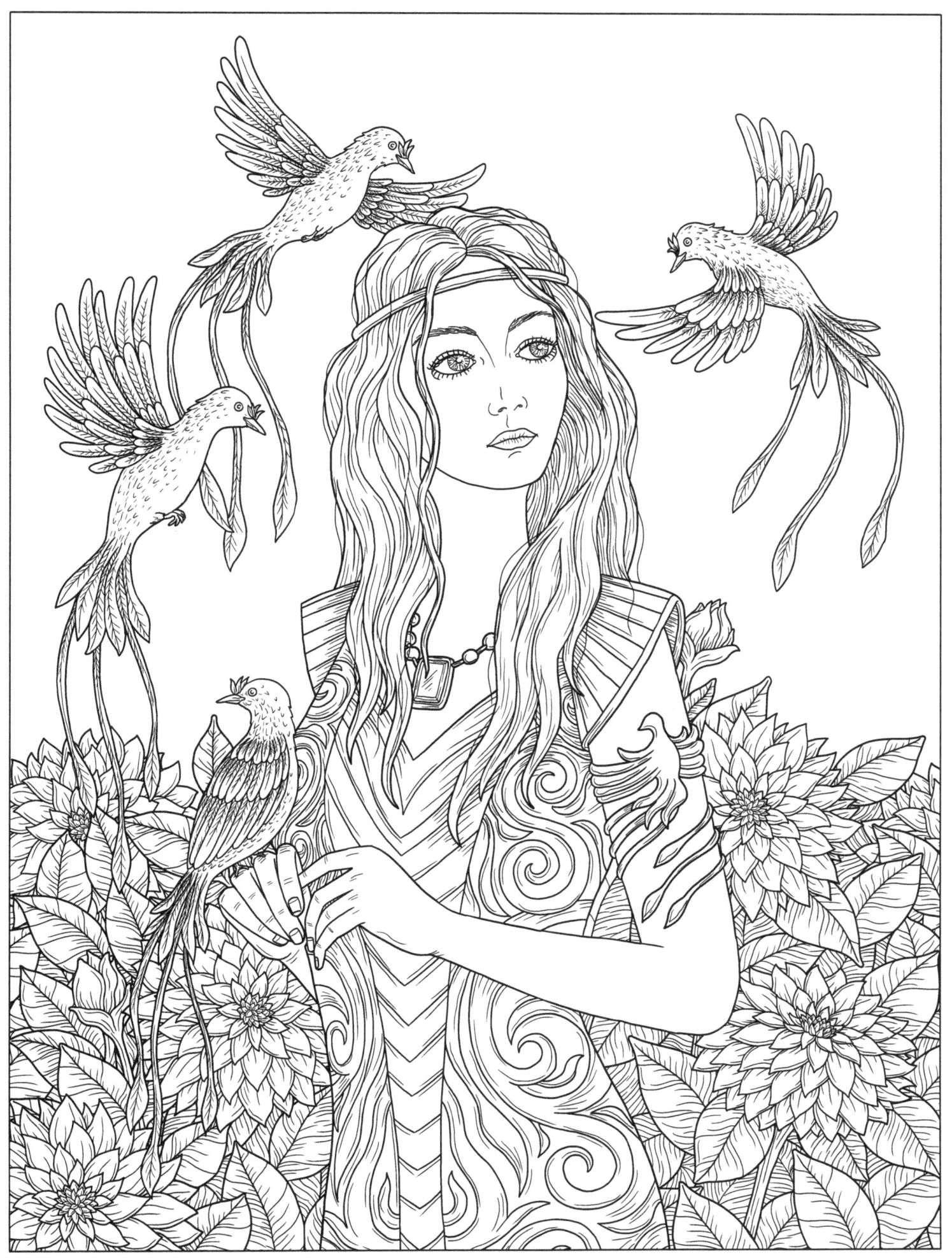

Dragon Healer

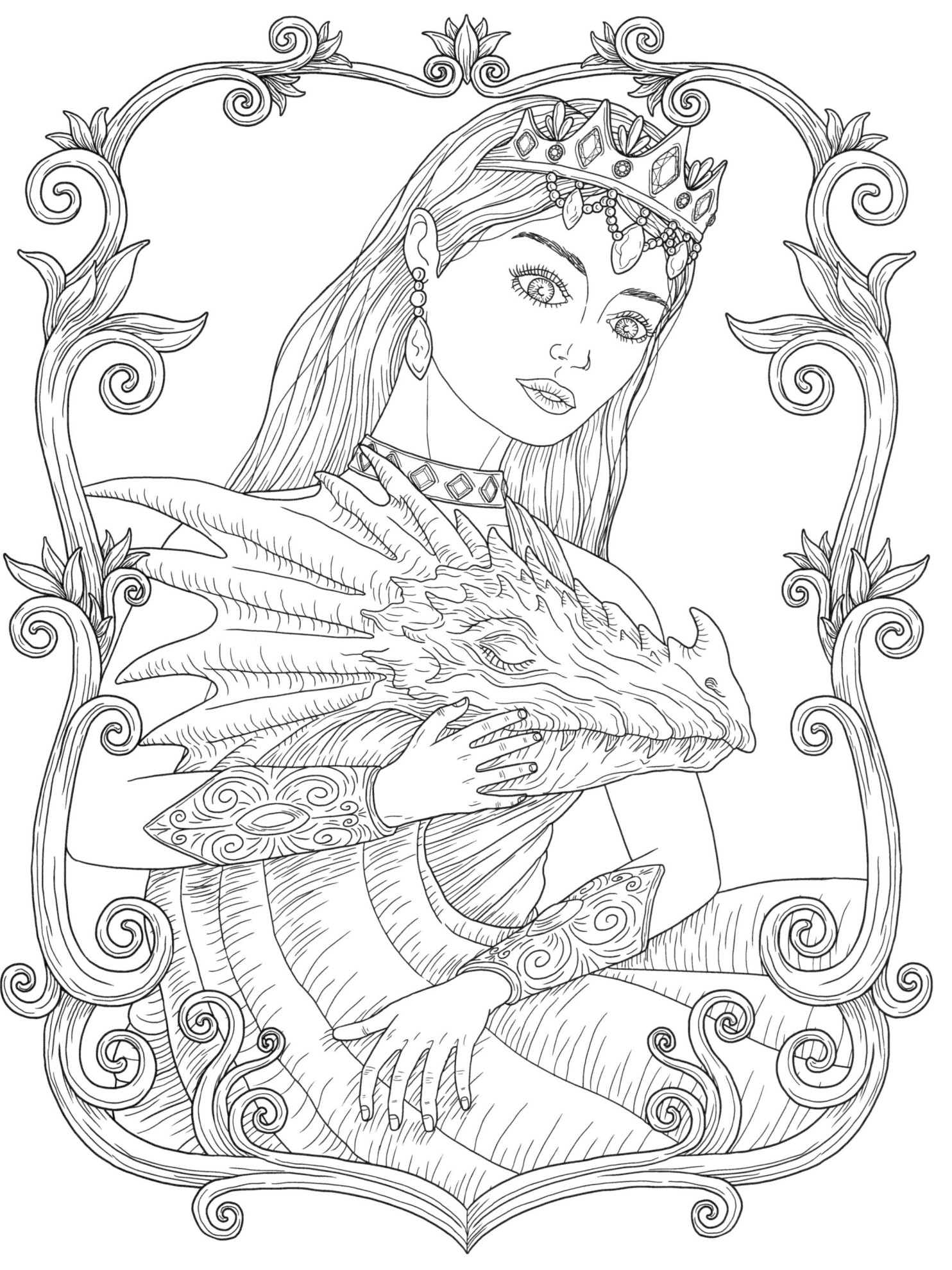

Jewel Prospector

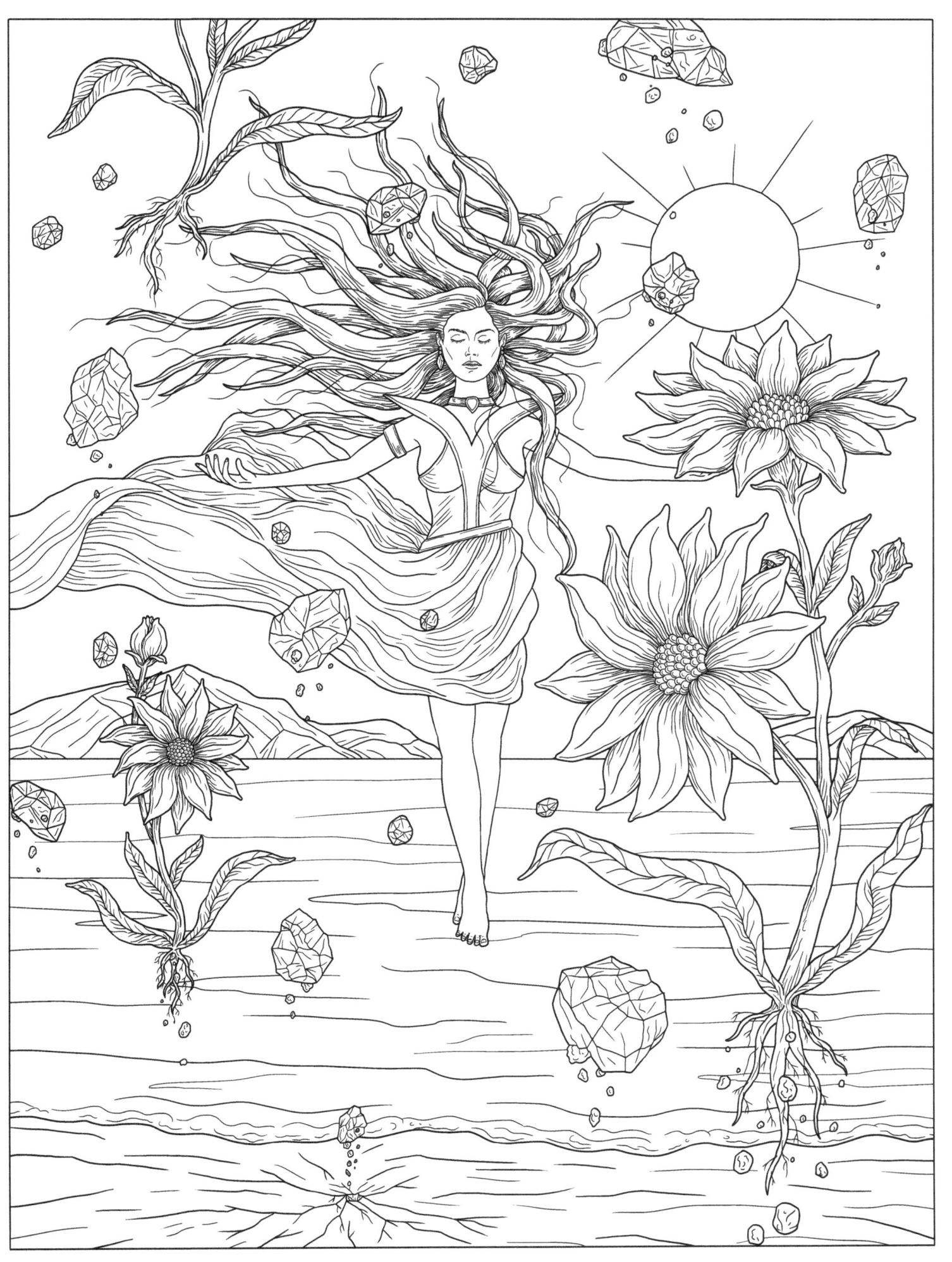

The Longing

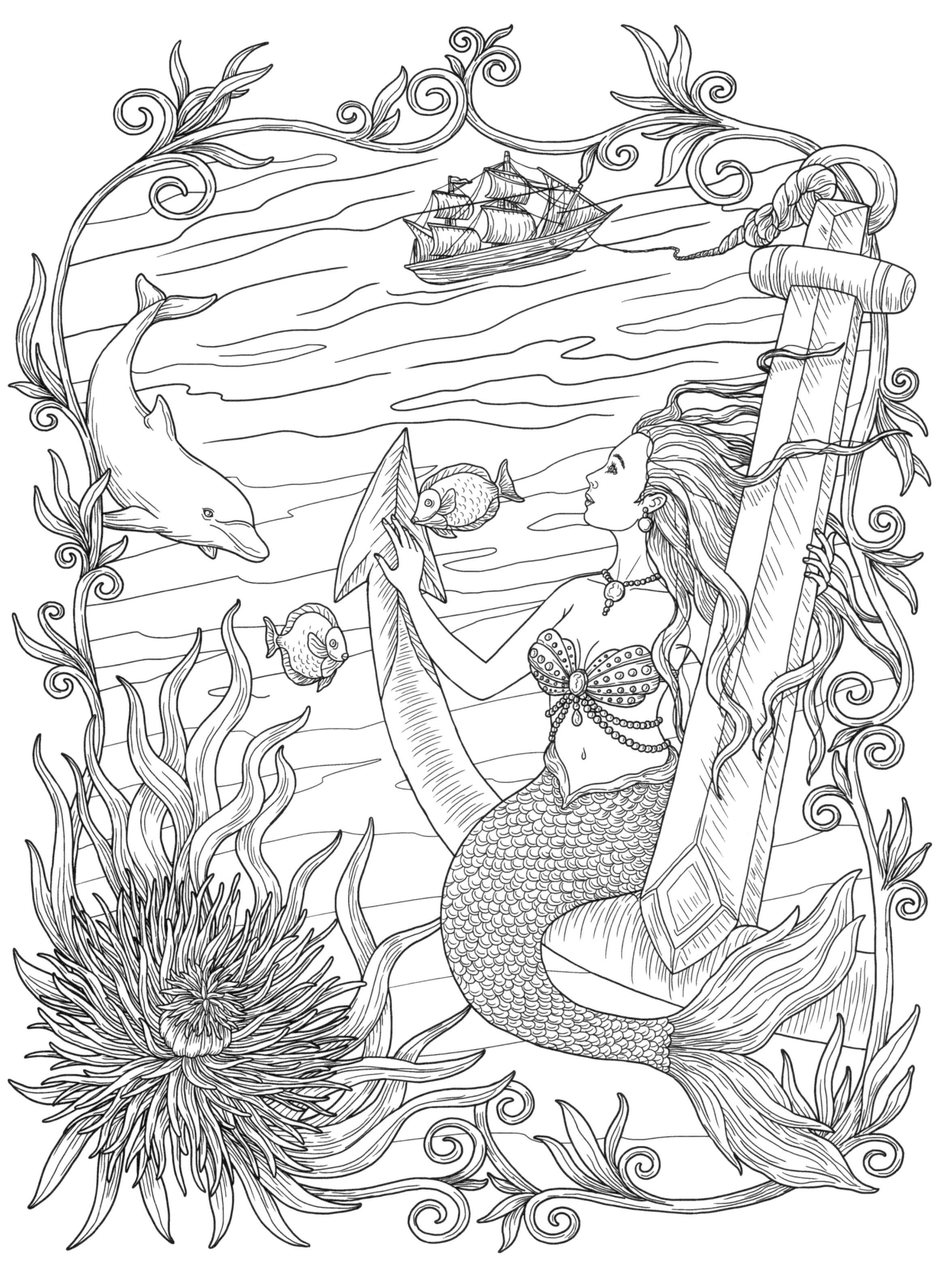

Enter Eden

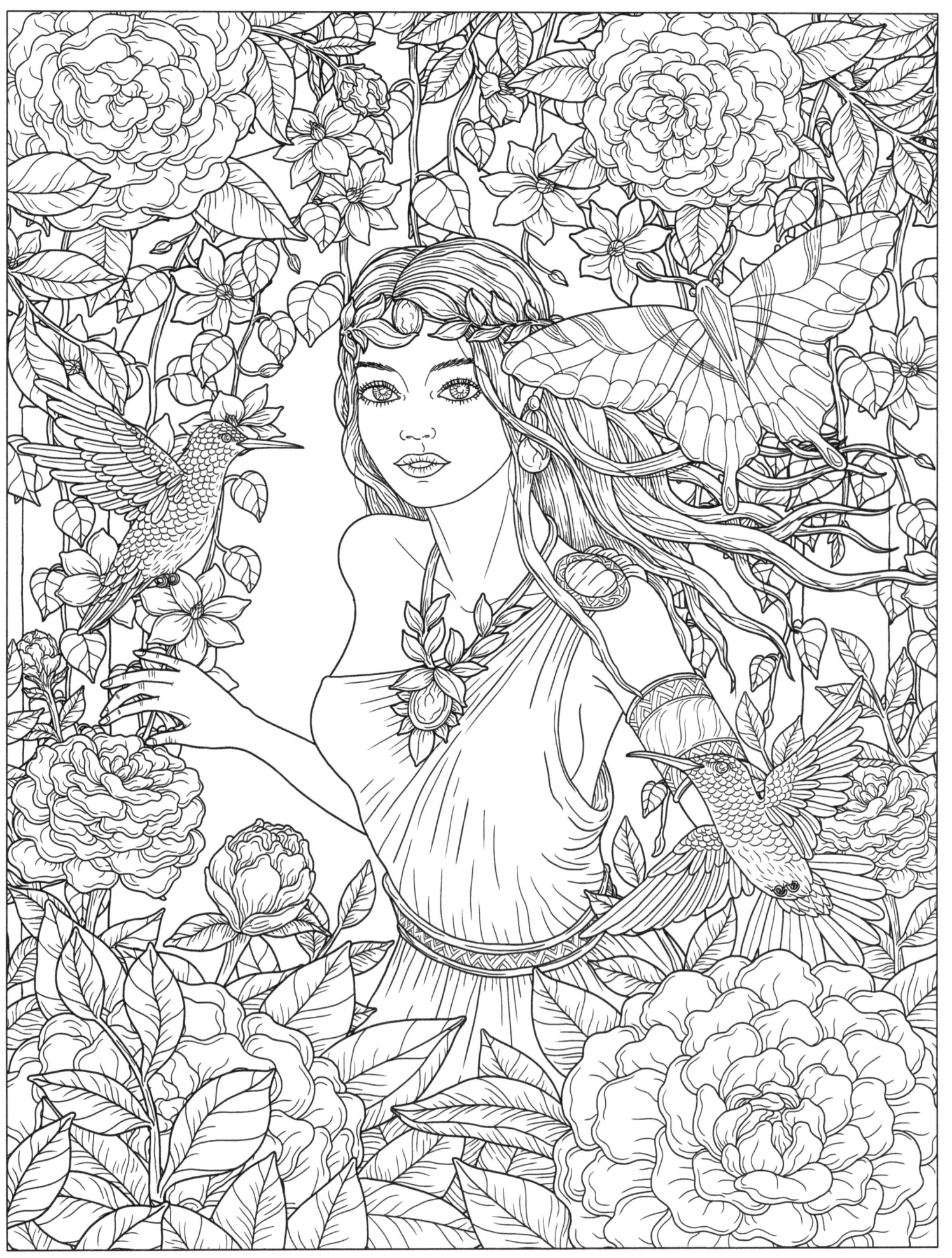

ALSO AVAILABLE
FROM VIVID PUBLISHERS

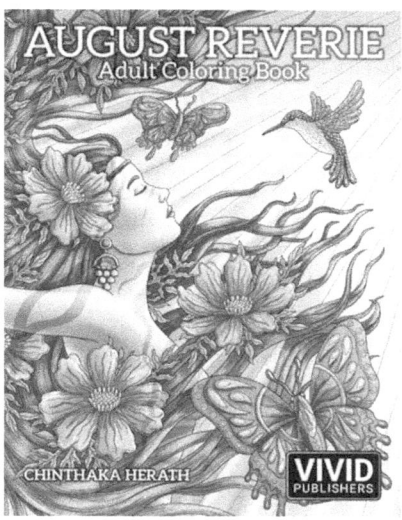

August Reverie

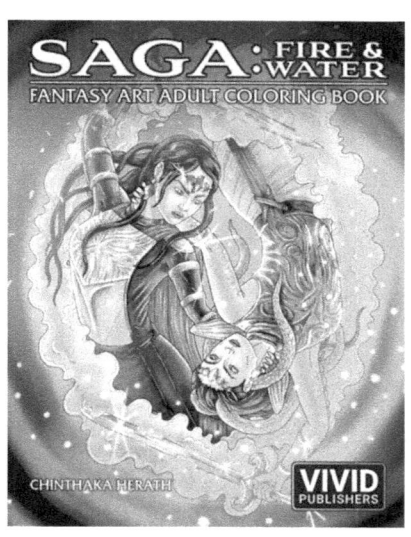

Saga: Fire & Water

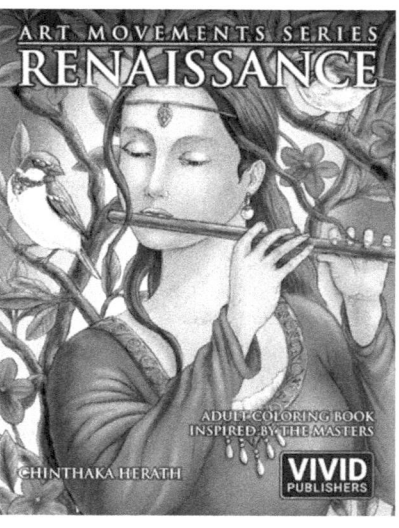

Art Movements Series:
Renaissance

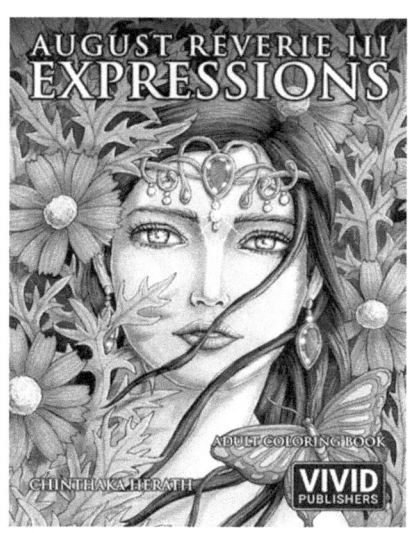

August Reverie 3:
Expressions

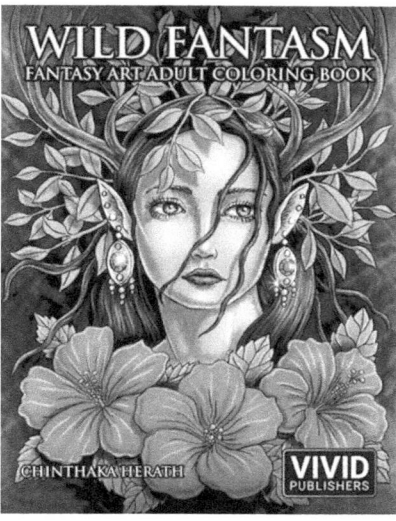

Wild Fantasm

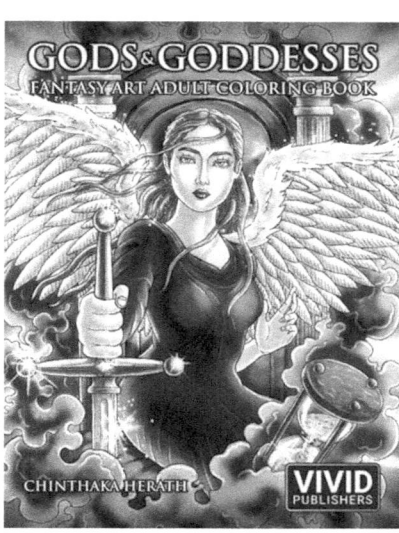

Gods & Goddesses